THE TRUTH ABOUT

forgiveness

THE TRUTH ABOUT

forgiveness

John MacArthur

THOMAS NELSON
Since 1798

NASHVILLE   DALLAS   MEXICO CITY   RIO DE JANEIRO

Published in Nashville, Tennessee, by Thomas Nelson. Thomas Nelson is a registered trademark of Thomas Nelson, Inc.

Thomas Nelson, Inc., titles may be purchased in bulk for educational, business, fund-raising, or sales promotional use. For information, please e-mail SpecialMarkets@ThomasNelson.com.

Unleashing God's Truth, One Verse at a Time® is a trademark of Grace to You. All rights reserved.

Compiled from previously published material in *The Jesus You Can't Ignore*, *The Vanishing Conscience*, *Hard to Believe*, *The Prodigal Son*, and *Welcome to the Family*.

Unless otherwise indicated, Scripture quotations are taken from THE NEW KING JAMES VERSION. © 1982 by Thomas Nelson, Inc. Used by permission. All rights reserved.

Scripture quotations marked NASB are taken from the NEW AMERICAN STANDARD BIBLE®. © The Lockman Foundation 1960, 1962, 1963, 1968, 1971, 1972, 1973, 1975, 1977, 1995. Used by permission.

Scripture quotations marked KJV are taken from the King James Version.

Library of Congress Cataloging-in-Publication Data

MacArthur, John, 1939-
  The truth about forgiveness / John MacArthur.
    p. cm.
  Includes bibliographical references (p.   ).
  ISBN 978-1-4002-0415-1
1. Forgiveness of sin. 2. Forgiveness--Religious aspects--Christianity. I. Title.
  BT795.M28 2012
  234'.5—dc23

Printed in the United States of America

12 13 14 15 16 QG 6 5 4 3 2 1

CONTENTS

CONTENTS

CHAPTER 1

WE NEED TO BE
FORGIVEN

THE BAD NEWS

Thousands of babies are born every day into a world filled with bad news. The term *bad news* has become a colloquialism to describe our era.

Why is there so much bad news? It's simple. The bad news that occurs on a larger scale is only the multiplication of what is occurring on an individual level. The power that makes for bad news is sin.

THE WORSE NEWS

A common contemporary response to this bad news is to deny it or try to explain it away. Perhaps the most prevalent means of escaping blame is by classifying every human failing as some kind of disease. Drunkards and drug addicts can check into clinics for treatment of their "chemical dependencies." Children who habitually defy authority can escape condemnation by being labeled "hyperactive" or having ADD (attention deficit disorder). Gluttons are no longer blameworthy; they suffer from an "eating disorder." Even the man who throws away his family's livelihood to pay for prostitutes is supposed to be an object of compassionate understanding; he is "addicted to sex."

An FBI agent was fired after he embezzled two thousand dollars, then gambled it away in a single afternoon at a casino. Later he sued, arguing that his gambling addiction was a disability, so his firing was an act of illegal discrimination. He won the case! Moreover, his therapy for the gambling addiction had to be funded under his employer's health-care insurance, just as if he had been suffering from appendicitis or an ingrown toenail.[1]

These days everything wrong with humanity is likely to be explained as an illness. What we used to call sin is more easily diagnosed as a whole array of disabilities. All kinds of immorality and evil conduct are now identified as symptoms of this or that psychological illness. Criminal behavior, various perverse passions, and every imaginable addiction have all been made excusable by the crusade to label them medical afflictions. Even commonplace problems, such as emotional weakness, depression, and anxiety, are also almost universally defined as quasi-medical, rather than spiritual, afflictions.

The American Psychiatric Association publishes a thick book to help therapists in the diagnosis of these new diseases. *The Diagnostic and Statistical Manual of Mental Disorders* (Third Edition, Revised)—or DSM-III-R, as it is popularly labeled—lists the following "disorders":

- *Conduct Disorder*—"a persistent pattern of conduct in which the basic rights of others and major age-appropriate societal norms or rules are violated."
- *Oppositional Defiant Disorder*—"a pattern of negativistic, hostile, and defiant behavior."
- *Histrionic Personality Disorder*—"a pervasive pattern of excessive emotionality and attention-seeking."
- *Antisocial Personality Disorder*—"a pattern of irresponsible and antisocial behavior beginning in childhood or early adolescence and continuing into adulthood."

And there are dozens more like those. Multitudes of parents, influenced by such diagnoses, refuse to punish their children for misbehavior. Instead, they seek therapy for ODD, or HDP, or whatever new diagnosis fits the unruly child's behavior.

In the words of one author, the disease-model approach to human behavior has so overwhelmed us as a society that we have gone haywire. We want to pass laws to excuse compulsive gamblers when they embezzle money to gamble and to force insurance companies to pay to treat them. We want to treat people who can't find love and who instead (when they are women) go after dopey, superficial men or (when they are men) pursue endless sexual liaisons without finding true happiness. And we want to call all these things—and many, many more—addictions.

What is this new addiction industry meant to accomplish? More and more addictions are being discovered, and new addicts are being identified, until all of us will be locked into our own little addictive worlds with other addicts like ourselves, defined by the special interests of our neuroses. What a repugnant world to imagine, as well as a hopeless one. Meanwhile, all the addictions we define are increasing.[2]

Worse yet, the number of people who suffer from such newly identified "sicknesses" is increasing even faster. The therapy industry is clearly not solving the problem of what Scripture calls sin. Instead it merely convinces multitudes that they are desperately sick and therefore not really responsible for their wrong behavior. It gives them permission to think of themselves as patients, not malefactors. And it encourages them to undergo extensive—and expensive—treatment that lasts for years, or better yet, for a lifetime. These new diseases, it seems, are ailments from which no one is ever expected to recover completely.

The sin-as-disease model has proved to be a boon to the multibillion-dollar counseling industry, and the shift toward long-term or even permanent therapy promises a bright economic future for professional therapists. One psychologist who has analyzed this trend suggests there is a clear strategy to the way therapists market their services:

1. Continue the psychologization of life;
2. Make problems out of difficulties and spread the alarm;
3. Make it acceptable to have the problem and be unable to resolve it on one's own;
4. Offer salvation [psychological, not spiritual].[3]

He notes that many therapists purposely extend their treatments over periods of many years, even after the original problem that provoked the client to seek counseling has been solved or forgotten. "They go on for so long and the client becomes so dependent on the therapist that a special period of time—sometimes extending to six months or more—is required to get the client ready to leave."[4]

Even commonplace problems, such as emotional weakness, depression, and anxiety, are also almost universally defined as quasi-medical, rather than spiritual, afflictions.

Recovery, the code word for programs modeled after Alcoholics Anonymous, is explicitly marketed as a lifelong program. We've grown accustomed to the image of a person who has been sober for forty years standing up in an AA meeting and saying, "I'm Bill, and I'm an alcoholic." Now all "addicts" are using the same approach—including sex addicts, gambling addicts, nicotine addicts, anger addicts, wife-beating addicts, child-molesting addicts, debt addicts, self-abuse addicts, envy addicts, failure addicts, overeating addicts, or whatever. People suffering from such maladies are taught to speak of themselves as "recovering," never "recovered." Those who dare to think of themselves as delivered from their affliction are told they are living in denial.

THE WRONG PRESCRIPTION

Disease-model therapy therefore feeds the very problem it is supposed to treat. It alleviates any sense of guilt, while making people feel they are victims, helplessly bound for life to their affliction. Is it any wonder that such a diagnosis so often becomes a self-fulfilling prophecy?

Misdiagnosis means any prescribed treatment will be utterly ineffective. The care indicated for conditions labeled pathological usually involves long-term therapy, self-acceptance, a recovery program, or all of the above—perhaps even with some other psychological gimmick such as self-hypnosis thrown in to complete the elixir. "In place of evil, therapeutic society has substituted 'illness'; in place of consequence, it urges therapy and understanding; in place of responsibility, it argues for a personality driven by impulses. The illness excuse has become almost routine in cases of public misconduct."[5]

But assume for the moment that the problem is sin rather than sickness. The only true remedy involves humble repentance and confession (the recognition that you deserve the chastening of God because you alone are responsible for your sin)—then restitution, and growth through the spiritual disciplines of prayer, Bible study, communion with God, fellowship with other believers, and dependence on Christ. In other words, if the problem is in fact spiritual, labeling it a clinical issue will only exacerbate the problem and will offer no real deliverance from the sin. That is precisely what we see happening everywhere.

The sad truth is that disease-model treatment is disastrously counterproductive. By casting the sinner in the role of a victim, it ignores or minimizes the personal guilt inherent in the misbehavior. "I am sick" is much easier to say than, "I have sinned." But it doesn't deal with the fact that one's transgression is a serious offense against a holy, omniscient, omnipotent God.

Personal guilt is for that very reason at the heart of what must be confronted when dealing with one's sin. But the disease-model remedy cannot address the problem of guilt without explaining it away. And by explaining guilt away, disease-model therapy does untold violence to the human conscience. It is therefore no remedy at all, but a disastrous prescription for escalating wickedness and eternal damnation.

One might think that victimism and disease-model therapy are so obviously contrary to biblical truth that Bible-believing Christians would rise up en masse and expose the error of such thinking. But tragically, that has not been the case. Victimism has become almost as influential within the evangelical church as it is in the unbelieving world, thanks to self-esteem theology and the church's fascination with worldly psychology.

These days, when sinners seek help from churches and other Christian agencies, they are likely to be told that their problem is some emotional disorder or psychological syndrome. They might be encouraged to forgive themselves and told they ought to have more self-love and self-esteem. They are not as likely to hear that they must repent and humbly seek God's forgiveness in Christ. That is such an extraordinary change of direction for the church that even secular observers have noticed it.

Wendy Kaminer, for example, does not purport to be a Christian. If anything, she seems hostile toward the church. She describes herself as "a skeptical, secular humanist, Jewish, feminist, intellectual lawyer."[6]

But she has seen the change of direction within evangelicalism, and she describes it with uncanny precision. She notes that religion and psychology have always more or less deemed each other incompatible. Now she sees "not just a truce but a remarkable accommodation."[7] Even from her perspective as an unbeliever, she can see that this accommodation has meant a wholesale alteration of the fundamental message about sin and salvation. She wrote:

> Christian codependency books, like those produced by the Minirth-Meier clinic in Texas, are practically indistinguishable from codependency books published by secular writers. . . . Religious writers justify their reliance on psychology by praising it for "catching up" to some eternal truths, but they've also found a way to make the temporal truths of psychology palatable. Religious leaders once condemned psychoanalysis for its moral neutrality. . . . Now popular religious literature equates illness with sin.[8]

Some of the criticism Kaminer levels against evangelicals is unwarranted or misguided, but in this respect, she is right on target: the inevitable result of Christians' embracing secular psychology has been the abandonment of any coherent concept of sin. And that has inevitably clouded the message we proclaim.

Describing the prevailing spirit of our age, Kaminer wrote, "No matter how bad you've been in the narcissistic 1970s and the acquisitive 1980s, no matter how many drugs you've ingested, or sex acts performed, or how much corruption enjoyed, you're still essentially innocent: the divine child inside you is always untouched by the worst of your sins."[9]

Elsewhere, she said,

> Inner children are always good—innocent and pure—like the most sentimentalized Dickens characters, which means that people are essentially good. . . . Even Ted Bundy had a child within. Evil is merely a mask—a dysfunction.
>
> The therapeutic view of evil as sickness, not sin, is strong in co-dependency theory—it's not a fire and brimstone theology. "Shaming" children, calling them bad, is considered a primary form of abuse. Both guilt and shame "are not useful as a way of life," Melody Beattie writes earnestly in *Codependent No More*. "Guilt makes *everything* harder. . . . We need to forgive ourselves" [(New York: Harper & Row, 1989), pp. 114–115]. Someone should remind Beattie that there's a name for people who lack guilt and shame: sociopaths. We ought to be grateful if guilt makes things like murder and moral corruption "harder."[10]

Ms. Kaminer suggests that evangelicalism has been infiltrated by this new anthropology-psychology-theology, and that it is antithetical to what we ought to believe and teach about sin. In that regard she surely understands more than the horde of evangelical writers who continue to echo themes from the secular self-esteem cult.

This is a serious matter. Whether you deny sin overtly and openly and totally, or covertly and by implication, any tampering with the biblical concept of sin makes chaos of the Christian faith.

Those ubiquitous phone-in counseling programs on Christian radio may provide one of the best barometers of popular Christianity's trends. When was the last time you heard an on-the-air counselor tell someone suffering from conscience pangs, "Your guilt is valid; you are sinful and must seek full repentance before God"?

Recently I listened to a talk show on a local religious radio station. This daily program features a man who bills himself as a Christian psychologist. On the day I listened he was talking about the importance of overcoming our sense of guilt. Self-blame, he told his audience, is usually irrational and therefore potentially very harmful. He gave a long lecture about the importance of forgiving oneself. The whole discourse was an echo of the world's wisdom: Guilt is a virtual mental defect. Don't let it ruin your self-image.

And so on. He never mentioned repentance or restitution as prerequisites for self-forgiveness, and he never cited a single passage of Scripture.

That kind of counsel is as deadly as it is unbiblical. Guilt feelings may not always be rational, but they are nearly always a reliable signal that something is wrong somewhere, and we had better come to grips with whatever it is and make it right. Guilt functions in the spiritual realm like pain in the material realm. Pain tells us there is a physical problem that must be dealt with or the body will suffer harm. Guilt is a spiritual pain in the soul that tells us something is evil and needs to be confronted and cleansed.

To deny personal guilt is to sacrifice the soul for the sake of the ego. Besides, disavowal doesn't really deal with guilt, as we all know intuitively. Far from having beneficial results, it destroys the conscience, and thereby weakens a person's ability to avoid destructive sin. Furthermore, it actually renders a healthy self-image altogether unattainable. "How can we have self-respect if we are not responsible for what we are?"[11] More important, how can we have true self-respect without hearty approval from a healthy conscience?

From a *biblical* perspective, that kind of counsel can be spiritually destructive. It fails to address the real problem of human sinfulness. It feeds the worst tendencies of human nature. It engenders the most catastrophic form of denial—denial of one's own guilt. And for most, who can't really shake the guilt, it adds more guilt for blaming someone who isn't really to blame at all.

Disavowing our personal culpability can never free us from a sense of guilt. On the contrary, those who refuse to acknowledge their sinfulness actually place themselves in bondage to their own guilt. "He that covereth his sins shall not prosper: but whoso confesseth and forsaketh them shall have mercy" (Proverbs 28:13 KJV). "If we say that we have no sin, we are deceiving ourselves, and the truth is not in us. [But] if we confess our sins, He is faithful and righteous to forgive us our sins and to cleanse us from all unrighteousness" (1 John 1:8–9).

Jesus Christ came into the world to save sinners! Jesus specifically said He had not come to save those who want to exonerate themselves (Mark 2:17). Where there is no recognition of sin and guilt, when the conscience has been abused into silence, there can be no salvation, no sanctification, and therefore no real emancipation from sin's ruthless power.

THE GOOD NEWS

With so much bad news, can there really be any good news? Yes! The good news is that sin can be dealt with. You don't have to be selfish. Guilt and anxiety can be alleviated. There is meaning to life and hope of life after death. The apostle Paul says in Romans 1:1 that the good news is the gospel. It is the good news that man's sin can be forgiven, guilt can be removed, life can have meaning, and a hopeful future can be a reality.

We Cannot Atone for Our Own Sin

The Old Testament never once suggested that sinners could atone for their own sin (either wholly or even in part) by doing good works or performing elaborate rituals. In fact, the dominant picture of atonement in the Old Testament is that of an innocent substitute whose blood was shed on behalf of the sinner.

The shedding of the substitute's blood was perhaps the single most prominent aspect of atonement for sin. "Without shedding of blood there is no remission" (Hebrews 9:22). On the Day of Atonement, the blood of the sin offering was deliberately splashed onto everything in the vicinity of the altar. The priest "sprinkled with blood both the tabernacle and all the vessels of the ministry. And according to the law almost all things are purified with blood" (vv. 21–22)—the worshipper included.

This was not to suggest that the blood itself had some kind of magical, mystical, or metaphysical property that literally washed away sin's defilement. But the purpose of this bloody ritual was simple: the blood everywhere made a vivid—and intentionally revolting—illustration of the fearsome reality that the wages of sin is death. "For the life of the flesh is in the blood, and I have given it to you upon the altar to make atonement for your souls; for it is the blood that makes atonement for the soul" (Leviticus 17:11).

By definition, then, no sinner can ever fully atone for his or her own sin, and that is why Scripture so frequently stresses the need for a substitute.

We Need a Substitute

When Abraham was told to sacrifice Isaac on an altar, for example, God Himself supplied a substitute in the form of a ram to be slain in Isaac's place. At Passover, the substitute was a spotless lamb. The main staple of the sacrificial system under Moses' law was the burnt offering, which could be a young bull, lamb, goat, turtledove, or pigeon (depending on the financial abilities of the worshipper). And once a year, on the Day of Atonement, the high priest sacrificed a bull and a goat, along with an additional burnt offering, as a symbol of atonement—a substitute who suffered for the sins of all the people.

Now it should be obvious to anyone that "it is not possible that the blood of bulls and goats could take away sins" (Hebrews 10:4; see Micah 6:6–8). That's why the ritual sacrifices had to be repeated daily. Everyone who ever seriously thought about the sacrificial system and weighed the real cost of sin had to face this truth eventually: animal sacrifices simply could not provide a full and final atonement for sin. Something more needed to be done to make a full atonement.

There were basically two possible answers to the dilemma. One approach was to adopt a system of merit such as the Pharisees' religion, in which the sinner himself tried to embellish or supplement the atoning significance of the animal sacrifices with several more layers of good works. In the Pharisees' case, this seems to be the very reason they made up their own long list of exacting rules and regulations that went so far beyond what the Law actually required. They knew very well that simple obedience to the Law couldn't possibly be perfect and therefore could never achieve enough merit to atone for sin. So they artificially supplemented what the Law required, thinking that their extra works would enable them to gain supplemental merit. The inevitable result was a system that promoted the most blatant forms of self-righteousness while diminishing the proper role of true faith.

The other approach was the one followed by every truly faithful person from the beginning of time until the coming of Christ. They acknowledged their own inability to atone for sin, embraced God's promise of forgiveness, and trusted Him to send a Redeemer who would provide a full and final atonement (Isaiah

59:20). From the day when Adam and Eve ate the forbidden fruit and their race was cursed, faithful believers had looked for the promised offspring of the woman who would finally crush the serpent's head and thus put sin and guilt away forever (Genesis 3:15). Despite some very strong hints (including Daniel 9:24 and Isaiah 53:10), the actual means by which redemption would finally be accomplished remained shrouded in mystery, until Jesus Himself explained it after His resurrection to some disciples on the road to Emmaus (Luke 24:27).

CHAPTER 2

GOD ALONE CAN FORGIVE SIN

In Luke 5:17–26, we find the story of Jesus healing the paralyzed man who had been lowered to Him through the roof, by his friends.

THE PHARISEES

When Luke first mentions the "Pharisees and teachers of the law," they are watching Jesus from the sidelines. They have come to Capernaum, not as part of the normal crowd seeking to benefit from Jesus' ministry, but as critical observers, looking for reasons to condemn Him and if possible thwart Him before He became any more popular. It is clear that they had formed this agenda ahead of time, because they arrived "on a certain day . . . out of every town of Galilee, Judea, and Jerusalem" (5:17).

Jesus was in Capernaum, in a house. Mark seems to suggest that it was the house where Jesus Himself lived (2:1). As usual, the press of the crowds was suffocating, and Jesus was preaching from within the house to as many people as could gather within earshot. Mark describes the scene: "Many were gathered together, so that there was no longer room, not even near the door; and He was speaking the word to them" (2:2 NASB). Luke adds, "And the power of the Lord was present to heal them" (5:17).

Here's a pattern you will notice in almost every confrontation between Jesus and the Pharisees: in one way or another, His deity is always at the heart of the conflict. It is as if He deliberately provokes them with claims, statements, or actions that He knows they will object to, and then He uses the resulting conflict to demonstrate that all the authority He claimed did indeed belong to Him.

On this occasion, the issue at stake was the forgiveness of sins. Remember that Jesus had been performing public healings for several weeks all over Galilee. There was no question about His ability to heal any disease or deliver the spiritually downtrodden from any kind of demonic bondage. Demons and disease alike always fled at His Word—sometimes even at His presence. "Wherever He entered, into villages, cities, or the country, they laid the sick in the marketplaces, and begged Him that they might just touch the hem of His garment. And as many as touched Him were made well" (Mark 6:56). In Jesus' own words, this was the proof of all His claims and the confirmation of all His teaching: "The blind see, the lame walk, the lepers are cleansed, the deaf hear, the dead are raised, the poor have the gospel preached to them" (Luke 7:22).

On this particular day, however, Jesus was presented with a particularly difficult case—a tragic and incurable affliction so debilitating that the sick man had to be carried on a stretcher by four other men. The crowd was so concentrated and so tightly drawn to Jesus in order to hear, it would have been well nigh impossible for one healthy man to squeeze through and get next to Jesus, much less four men carrying a paraplegic on a stretcher.

Here was a man so desperately in need of healing that four others—perhaps friends and neighbors, possibly even relatives—had gone to all this trouble to carry him to Capernaum in order to seek help from this healer they had all heard about. But when they got there, there was no hope of even seeing Jesus, because the spiritually starved multitudes essentially had Him barricaded in a house, from which His voice could only faintly be heard teaching.

It may well be that forgiveness was the very topic He was teaching about. The subject was certainly in the air. Immediately before this, after teaching from Peter's boat, Jesus had instructed Peter to launch out into the deep and let down his nets (Luke 5:4). To any fisherman, such a strategy would sound foolish. Fish were best netted at night, in shallow waters, while they were feeding. Peter had fished all night and caught nothing (v. 5). During daylight hours, the fish would migrate to much deeper, cooler waters, where it would normally be impossible to reach them with nets.

"Nevertheless," Peter said, "at Your word I will let down the net" (v. 5). When the haul of fishes was so great that the nets began to break, Peter was instantly smitten with the realization that he was in the presence of divine power—and the first thing he was aware of was the weight of his own guilt. "He fell down at Jesus' knees, saying, 'Depart from me, for I am a sinful man, O Lord!'" (v. 8).

Forgiveness was also one of Jesus' favorite subjects to preach about. It was one of the key themes in His Sermon on the Mount. It was a focus of the Lord's Prayer and the subject He expounded on at the end of that prayer (Matthew 6:14–15). It's the central theme that dominates all of Luke 5. If forgiveness was not the very subject Jesus was preaching on, it was nevertheless about to become the topic of the day.

Now imagine the Pharisees, sitting somewhere on the periphery, watching and listening for things to criticize as these four men carrying the stretcher arrived on the scene.

THE MAN

If they wanted to see Jesus in action, these Pharisees had certainly come on the right day. Here was a hopelessly paralyzed man who had been brought from some distance by four other men whose journey from another village could not have been an easy one. And when they arrived, they must have seen instantly that they had no hope of getting close to Jesus by any conventional method. Even if they waited until Jesus left the house, the crowds were much too thick and too electrified to make way for five men to penetrate all the way to the center of the vast throng that surrounded Jesus wherever He went.

The fact that the man was carried on a pallet rather than seated in some kind of cart suggests that he was probably a quadriplegic, totally paralyzed in all his limbs—perhaps as a result of some injury to his neck. He was a classic object lesson about the fallen human condition. He was unable to move, utterly reliant on the grace and goodness of others, completely impotent to do anything whatsoever for himself.

Here was an infirmity that would require a true and obvious miracle for healing. This was not like the invisible ailments (sore backs, migraines, and stomach ailments) we often see "cured" by people who claim to possess gifts of healing today. His muscles would be atrophied and shriveled to nothing from nonuse. If Jesus could heal him, it would be instantly obvious to all that a true miracle had taken place.

The sheer desperation of the man and his four friends can be measured by what they did when they realized they would not be able to get close to Jesus. They went up to the roof. In order for four men to ascend with a stretcher, there must have been an external stairway leading to a veranda or walkway. Even at that, it would be a difficult ascent. But this was evidently a substantial house, with a typical Mediterranean-style upper-level patio adjacent to a tiled section of roof. That afforded the men exactly the opportunity they needed. They carried the man upstairs, determined approximately where Jesus was below them, and began removing the tiles over that part of the roof.

What a dramatic entrance this was! It no doubt startled the crowd when the roof began to open up. The gap in the roof needed to be large enough for the man and his stretcher—which likely meant that not only the external roof tiles but also some of the underlying latticework supporting the tiles had to be carefully removed. A tile roof was no cheap or temporary covering, and there's simply no way to open a hole in a tile roof like that without lots of debris and dust falling into the crowd below. We would normally expect both the crowd and the landlord to be annoyed by the actions of these men. But in Jesus' eyes, this was clear evidence of great faith.

All three Synoptic Gospels record this incident, and all three say Jesus "saw their faith" (Luke 5:20; Matthew 9:2; Mark 2:5). He saw faith reflected in their persistence and determination, of course. After all the work they had done to lay their friend at Jesus' feet, it was obvious to everyone what they were there for: they had brought the man for physical healing. Anyone who thought about it could see it required some degree of faith in Jesus' healing ability to go to all that work.

But the text is suggesting that Jesus saw something even deeper. Because He is God incarnate, He could also see into their hearts, perceive their motives, and even know their thoughts—just as He had seen into the heart of Nicodemus, and just as He had discerned the halfhearted faith of those early admirers of His ministry in Jerusalem to whom He had refused to commit Himself (John 2:23–25).

What He saw as these men lowered their friend from the ceiling was true faith—repentant faith. Not one of the gospel accounts suggests that either the paralyzed man or his friends said a word. There was no verbal testimony from the man about his repentance. There was no statement of contrition. There was no confession of sin. There was no affirmation of faith in God. There was no verbal cry for mercy. There didn't need to be; Jesus could see into the man's heart and mind. He knew that the Holy Spirit had done a work in the paralyzed man's heart. The man had come to Jesus with a broken and contrite spirit. He wanted to be right with God. He did not even need to say that. Jesus knew it because, as God, He knows all hearts.

THE MIRACLE

Here was an opportunity for Jesus to display His deity. Everyone could see the man's affliction; only Jesus could see his *faith*. Without any comment either from the paralytic man at Jesus' feet or from the four men peering through the hole in the roof, Jesus turned to the paralytic man and said, "Man, your sins are forgiven you" (Luke 5:20).

He freely forgave him. He fully justified him. With those words, the man's sins were obliterated from his account, wiped off the divine books. On His own personal authority, Jesus instantly absolved that man of all the guilt of all his sins forever.

THE REACTION

With that claim, Jesus gave the scribes and Pharisees exactly what they were waiting for: an opportunity to accuse Him. And make no mistake: Jesus' words to the paralytic would be deeply shocking to the Pharisees' religion by any measure. In the first place, if He were not God incarnate, it would indeed be the very height of blasphemy for Him to pretend He had authority to forgive sins. In the second place, the Pharisees' religion was strongly oriented toward works—so that in their view, forgiveness must be *earned*. It was unthinkable to them that forgiveness could ever be granted immediately and unconditionally by faith alone.

According to Matthew, some of the scribes who were there reacted "at once" (9:3). But curiously, in this instance, they did not rise up and shout out a verbal protest. It was still early enough in Jesus' ministry, and they constituted a small enough minority on the fringe of this crowd in Jesus' own community, that their initial reaction seems surprisingly subdued. If their shock registered at all, it was only on their faces.

Luke said they "began to reason, saying, 'Who is this who speaks blasphemies? Who can forgive sins but God alone?'" (5:21). Matthew made it clear that they said these things "within themselves"—not aloud (9:3). Mark likewise said, "The scribes were sitting there and reasoning in their hearts, 'Why does this Man speak blasphemies like this? Who can forgive sins but God alone?'" (2:6–7). In their minds collectively they were all thinking the same thing. *This is blasphemy of the worst kind. Who but God can legitimately forgive sins?*

The question was merely rhetorical; they weren't really wondering what the answer might be. They knew full well that no one can forgive sins except God. Their doctrine on that point was sound enough. You and I can individually forgive whatever wrongs are done to us as far as our own personal claims for justice are concerned, but we don't have the authority to absolve anyone from guilt before the throne of God. No man can do that. No priest can do that. No one can do that but God alone. Anyone who usurps that prerogative is either God or a blasphemer. In fact, for someone who is not God, this would indeed be the supreme act of blasphemous idolatry—putting himself in the place of God.

THE VERDICT

Jesus had deliberately put Himself at the center of a scenario that would force every observer to render a verdict about Him. That's true not only of the people who were eyewitnesses in Capernaum that day but also for those who simply read this account in Scripture. And the choice is clear. There are only two possible conclusions we can make with regard to Christ: He is either God incarnate, or He is a blasphemer and a fraud. There is no middle ground, and that is precisely the situation Jesus was aiming for.

There are a lot of people even today who want to patronize Jesus by saying He was a good person, an outstanding religious leader, an important prophet, a profound ethicist, a paragon of integrity, kindness, and decency—a great man, but still merely a man—not God incarnate. But this one episode in His public ministry is sufficient to erase that choice from the list of possibilities. He is either God or the ultimate blasphemer. He purposely erased every possible middle-way alternative.

Jesus did not scold the Pharisees for thinking that only God can forgive sin. They weren't wrong about that. Nor did He write their concern off as a misunderstanding of His intention. That's what He would have done if He were indeed a good man not claiming to be God incarnate, and not really claiming any special authority to forgive sin or justify sinners. If that were the case, He ought to have immediately said, "Whoa, whoa, whoa! You misunderstood me. I'm not saying I can forgive the man, I simply meant to say that God will forgive the man." Any good, noble, godly man would want to correct such a misconception and set the record straight, affirming that only God can forgive sin. He didn't do any of that.

Instead, He rebuked them for "think[ing] evil" about Him (Matthew 9:4). They were wrong to assume the worst about Him when in fact He had already often displayed the power of God convincingly and publicly by healing diseases that no one but God could heal and by casting out demons that only God has power over. Instead of thinking, *No mere man can forgive sin. He just blasphemed*, they ought to have been asking themselves, *Can it possibly be that this is no mere man?*

All three Synoptics stress that Jesus read their thoughts (Matthew 9:4; Mark 2:8; Luke 5:22). Just as He knew the heart of the paralytic and understood that the man's first concern was for the salvation of his soul, He knew the hearts of the Pharisees and understood that their only motive was to find a way to accuse Him. The fact that He knew what they were thinking ought to have been another clue to them that He was no mere man.

But they were already thinking well past that. As far as they were concerned, this was a case of blasphemy pure and simple, and no other option even seems to have occurred to them. Moreover, if they could make that accusation stick, they could call for Him to be stoned. Open blasphemy was a capital crime. Leviticus 24:16 was emphatic about that: "Whoever blasphemes the name of the LORD shall surely be put to death. All the congregation shall certainly stone him, the stranger as well as him who is born in the land. When he blasphemes the name of the LORD, he shall be put to death."

THE QUESTION

Before the scribes and Pharisees could even give voice to what they were thinking, Jesus Himself pressed the issue. "He answered and said to them, 'Why are you reasoning in your hearts? Which is easier, to say, "Your sins are forgiven you," or to say, "Rise up and walk"?'" (Luke 5:22–23).

They were thinking, *This man is blaspheming because he claims to do what only God can do.* Notice that Jesus did not even hint that they might have misunderstood His intentions. He did not double back and try to qualify His own statement. Nor did He challenge their belief that only God can forgive sin. As a matter of fact, they were exactly right about that.

Of course, only God can infallibly read human hearts too. In Ezekiel 11:5, God Himself says, "I know the things that come into your mind." He speaks again in Jeremiah 17:10: "I, the LORD, search the heart, I test the mind." No human has the ability to see perfectly into the mind of another like that. "The LORD does not see as man sees; for man looks at the outward appearance, but the LORD looks at the heart" (1 Samuel 16:7). Jesus had just displayed knowledge both of the paralytic's mind and their own secret thoughts about Him. Shouldn't that have made them pause and reflect on who this was that they were dealing with?

That is precisely what Jesus was challenging them to consider. He proposed a simple test: "Which is easier, to say, 'Your sins are forgiven you,' or to say, 'Rise up and walk'?" (Luke 5:23). While it is certainly true that only God can forgive sins, it is likewise true that only God can perform the kind of regenerative miracle necessary to restore the atrophied muscles and brittle bones of a quadriplegic to perfect wholeness in a split second—so that he could literally rise up and walk on command. The question was not whether Jesus could make this man better, but whether He could instantly make him whole and healthy.

Even with the best methods of modern medicine, if someone happens to recover the ability to move after suffering a catastrophic injury of the sort that causes severe paralysis, it usually takes months of therapy for the brain to rediscover how to send accurate signals through the injured nerve paths to the disabled limbs. Regardless of how long this man had been paralyzed, we might expect at the very least that he would need some time to learn how to walk again. But Jesus' healings always bypassed all such therapy. People born blind were given not only their sight but also the instant ability to make sense of what they saw (John 9:1–38; Mark 8:24–25). When Jesus healed a deaf person, He also immediately healed the resultant speech impediment—no therapy required (Mark 7:32–35). Whenever He healed lame people, He gave them not only regenerated muscle tissue but also the strength and dexterity to take up their beds and walk (Matthew 9:6; Mark 2:12).

It strikes me as ironic that when modern faith healers and charismatic charlatans nowadays claim to heal people, the patient usually falls over immobile, or in uncontrollable convulsions. Jesus' healings had exactly the opposite effect. Even a man infirm and bedridden for thirty-eight years could immediately pick up his pallet and walk away (John 5:6–9).

That is just what this man needed: an act of divine, creative power such as only God can perform.

Notice carefully the way Jesus framed His question: "Which is easier to say?" He was picking at their thought process. They were indignant because He had granted this man forgiveness. They had never challenged His right to heal. Obviously, both forgiveness and healing are impossible for any mere man to do. No mere man has the power either to heal at will or to absolve sin at will.

Healing is actually a perfect metaphor for forgiveness in that regard. In fact, the two things are inseparable, because sickness is a result of the curse brought on creation by sin. Sickness is merely a symptom; sin is the ultimate cause. (That's not to suggest that every sickness is the immediate consequence of a specific sin, of course. In John 9:3, Jesus expressly said there are other reasons for this or that individual's ailments. But the existence of illness and infirmity in a universe that was originally created perfect is nevertheless ultimately a result of the curse of sin.) So the power to heal all sickness presupposes the power to forgive any sin. Both are humanly impossible. But Jesus could do either or both with equal authority.

Still, which is easier to say? Obviously, it's easier to tell someone his sins are forgiven, because no one can see if it actually happened. The kind of forgiveness Jesus granted this man is a divine transaction. It occurs in the mind of God and the courtroom of heaven. It is a decree only God can make, and there's no immediate earthly evidence of it. It's easy to say; humanly impossible to do.

So Jesus in effect said, "You're questioning whether I can forgive that man's sin, aren't you? And you think it's very easy to say, 'Your sins are forgiven.' In fact, you think My saying it is blasphemy and that I have overstepped a boundary no man should ever come near."

The fact that Jesus knew their hearts so perfectly and yet refused to avert the public conflict they sought is significant. He knew full well that the Pharisees would be offended if He declared this man's sins forgiven, and yet He was not deterred from doing it. In fact, He did it as publicly as possible. He surely could have healed this man's infirmity without provoking that kind of open conflict with the Pharisees.

He could have also dealt privately with the issue of the man's guilt, rather than making such a pronouncement within earshot of everyone. Jesus was surely aware that many people in a crowd that size would not be able to understand what He was doing or why He did it. At the very least, He could have taken time to pause and explain why He had a right to exercise divine authority. Any or all of those things would have at least avoided the perception that He was deliberately inflaming the Pharisees.

Those are the kinds of things a typical, solicitous evangelical in these postmodern times might insist ought to be done. Shouldn't we avoid public controversy at all costs, especially in circumstances like these, with so many simple villagers present? Friction between Jesus and the religious elite of Israel could not possibly be edifying to the common fishermen and housewives of Capernaum, could it? A wise person would do everything in his power to avoid offending these Pharisees—right? What possible good could come from turning this man's deliverance into a theater of public controversy?

But Jesus had no such scruples. The point He was making was vastly more important than how the Pharisees or the people of Capernaum felt about it. Therefore, "'[So] that you may know that the Son of Man has power on earth to forgive sins'—He said to the man who was paralyzed, 'I say to you, arise, take up your bed, and go to your house'" (Luke 5:24).

Now, it is not at all easy to say to someone like this, "Arise, take up your bed, and go." Because if you say that and he doesn't do it straightaway, you have just revealed that you have no authority to do what you are claiming. Unlike the phony healings featured on religious television by today's celebrity faith healers,

Jesus' miracles involved serious and visible infirmities. He healed people who had suffered from appalling long-term maladies. He healed every imaginable kind of ailment—congenital disabilities and physical deformities included. He healed people as they came to Him—in their home towns and on their public streets—not from the safety of a stage surrounded by screeners and security guards. He performed countless healings—far more than those specifically described in Scripture (John 21:25)—healing everyone who ever came to Him for relief from any infirmity (Matthew 4:24; 12:15; 19:2; Mark 5:56; Luke 6:18–19). And He healed up close, in the presence of many eyewitnesses whose testimony could not possibly be impeached.

Impostors, fake healers, staged miracles, and counterfeit healings were as common in Jesus' time as they are today. So it is significant that no one ever seriously questioned the reality of Jesus' miracles—including the Pharisees. They always attacked Him on other grounds. They questioned the source of His power. They accused Him of wrongfully healing on the Sabbath. They would certainly have claimed He was merely using sleight of hand if a credible case for that accusation could have been made. But nothing in the gospel record suggests that the Pharisees or anyone else ever even tried accusing Him of fakery. How could they, given the nature and the abundance of His miracles?

Now His entire reputation hinged on an impossibility. He would demonstrate in the most graphic way possible that He has authority to do what only God can do.

THE CONCLUSION

Luke's account is notable for its straightforward simplicity. The writing style mirrors the startling suddenness of the miracle. Everything from this point on in the narrative happens so quickly that Luke covers it all in two short verses. Of the paralytic, Luke says, "*Immediately* he rose up before them, took up what he had been lying on, and departed to his own house, glorifying God" (5:25, emphasis added).

A lot happened in that one instant. The man's bones, fragile from nonuse, hardened perfectly. His muscles were restored at once to full strength and functionality. His joints and tendons became sturdy and mobile. All the elements of his physiology that had atrophied were regenerated. His nervous system switched back on and immediately became fully functional. Neuron fibers that had long ago ceased to feel anything sprang instantly back to life. One moment he felt nothing in those useless extremities; the next moment he felt all the strength and energy that comes with perfect health. Arms that one minute before had needed to be borne by four men and a stretcher sud-denly were able to carry the stretcher back home.

The man's departure seems awfully abrupt. But Jesus' command consisted of three simple impera-tives: "Arise, take up your bed, and go to your house" (v. 24). And that is precisely what the man did. If he paused to thank Jesus, he did not stop for long. We know for a fact that he was deeply grateful. But he was also understandably eager to get home and show his loved ones what God had done for him.

Luke doesn't say how far away his home was, but it must have been a wonderful walk. And here's where we see his profound gratitude: all the way home he was "glorifying God" (v. 25).

The Bible sometimes understates the obvious things: "glorifying God." That's what the angels did in heaven when they announced the birth of the Messiah (Luke 2:14–15). It's easy to envision this man running, leaping, clapping, and dancing all the way home. If his four friends went home with him, he probably outran them all. They must have been a little fatigued from carrying him to Capernaum; he was newly reborn, freshly invigorated, and relieved of every burden he had ever borne except that now-useless stretcher.

"Glorifying God" would also have involved lots of noise—laughing, shouting, and singing hallelujahs. I imagine he could hardly wait to run to his front door, throw it open with a shout of gladness, burst in with his new arms held wide, and celebrate his new wholeness with his wife, his kids, or whatever family he had at home.

But the *best* part was not that he could skip home; the best part was that he was cleansed of his sin. I don't know what all he had dared to hope for when he and the four erstwhile pallbearers started out that morning. But I'm fairly certain he did not expect what he got. All his sins were forgiven and he had been created new. No wonder he glorified God.

The miracle had a corresponding effect on the people of Capernaum. "They were all amazed, and they glorified God and were filled with fear, saying, 'We have seen strange things today!'" (Luke 5:26). The Greek expression Luke used means "seized with astonishment." The noun in that phrase is *ekstasis*, which of course is the root of the English word *ecstasy*. It literally speaks of a mind jolt—a powerful shock of amazement and profound delight. In this case, however, to translate the word as *ecstatic* would not really capture the people's reaction as Luke pictures it. It was more like stunned shock—mixed with fear and wonder.

Like the formerly paralyzed man, they glorified God. The praise of the crowd, however, is of a different character from the healed man's worship. He was moved by deep personal gratitude and a heart freshly delivered from guilt. They were simply in awe of the strangeness of what they had seen. We know from subsequent events that most of Capernaum's admiration for Jesus would turn out to be a fickle sort of esteem. Many in that crowd were halfhearted disciples and hangers-on who would quickly fall away when Jesus' teaching became harder.

But most peculiar is the fact that Luke says nothing more about the Pharisees. With a kind of stealth that will soon become a pattern, they simply lapse into utter silence and fade out of the story. The man who was healed went home one way, glorifying God and rejoicing in his newfound robe of righteousness. The religious leaders of Israel slunk away in the opposite direction—silently seething with anger, resentful that Jesus had pronounced the paralytic forgiven, unable even to rejoice in the man's good fortune, and silently plotting their next attempt to discredit Jesus. We know that was their response, because when they show up again, they will be a little more angry, a lot more exercised, and a lot less open to any serious consideration of Jesus' claims. This first Galilean controversy seems to mark the start of a pattern of increasingly hostile public conflicts with Jesus whereby their hearts would be completely hardened against Him.

This occasion also fairly summed up the spiritual reasons for the Pharisees' intense hatred of Jesus. They could not stand the compassion that would forgive a sinner on the spot. The idea that Jesus would instantly and freely justify a paralytic—someone who by definition was unable to work—contradicted everything they stood for. Jesus' exercise of divine authority also rankled them. It was not so much that they really believed Him guilty of blasphemy—after all, He answered that charge by repeatedly and convincingly proving He had full power to do what only God can do. But they had their own idea of what God should be like, and Jesus simply didn't fit the profile.

Besides all that, He was a threat to their status in Israel (John 11:48)—and the more He humiliated them in public this way, the more their own influence diminished. From here on, that reality loomed as an urgent crisis in all their thoughts about Him.

After this episode, critical Pharisees become commonplace in all the gospel narratives. They soon began to dog Jesus' steps everywhere He went, seizing every reason they could find to accuse Him, opposing Him at every turn, even resorting to lies and blasphemy in their desperation to discredit Him.

Clearly, if they would not acknowledge Him when they saw a dramatic miracle like the instant healing of this paralytic, nothing would penetrate their hardened, self-righteous hearts. They were already well down the path that would make them the chief conspirators in His murder.

Jesus, of course, embodied all the attributes of God—kindness, longsuffering, and mercy on the one hand; wrath, righteousness, and judgment on the other. All those qualities are discernible in some measure in the way He dealt with the Pharisees over the course of His ministry. But because the gospel was at stake and His own lordship was constantly under attack from these men who were the most influential spiritual leaders in the nation, His tenderness never overshadowed His severity in any of His dealings with them.

Their course was fixed, apparently sometime before this first Galilean encounter with Him. Their hearts were already set to be unyielding to His authority, oblivious to His teaching, opposed to His truth, insensitive to His righteousness, and impervious to His rebukes. They had essentially written Him off already.

He would soon write them off as well.

CHAPTER 3

GOD'S FORGIVENESS IS UNDESERVED

God's love to all humanity is a love of *compassion*. To say it another way, it is a love of pity. It is a brokenhearted love. He is "good, and ready to forgive, and abundant in lovingkindness to all who call upon [Him]" (Psalm 86:5 NASB). "To the Lord our God belong compassion and forgiveness, for we have rebelled against Him" (Daniel 9:9 NASB). He is "compassionate and gracious, slow to anger, and abounding in lovingkindness and truth" (Exodus 34:6 NASB). "God is love" (1 John 4:8, 16).

We must understand that there is nothing in any sinner that compels God's love. He does not love us because we are lovable. He is not merciful to us because we in any way deserve His mercy. We are despicable, vile sinners who, if we are not saved by the grace of God, will be thrown on the trash heap of eternity, which is hell. We have no intrinsic value, no intrinsic worth—there's nothing in us to love.

I recently overheard a radio talk-show psychologist attempting to give a caller an ego-boost: "God loves you for what you are. You *must* see yourself as someone special. After all, you are special to God." But that misses the point entirely. God *does not* love us "for what we are." He loves us *in spite of what we are*. He does not love us because we are special. Rather, it is only His love and grace that give our lives any significance at all.

That may seem like a doleful perspective to those raised in a culture where self-esteem is elevated to the supreme virtue. But it is, after all, precisely what Scripture teaches: "We have sinned like our fathers, we have committed iniquity, we have behaved wickedly" (Psalm 106:6 NASB). "All of us have become like one who is unclean, and all our righteous deeds are like a filthy garment; and all of us wither like a leaf, and our iniquities, like the wind, take us away" (Isaiah 64:6 NASB).

God loves because He is love; love is essential to who He is. Rather than viewing His love as proof of something worthy in us, we ought to be humbled by it.

God's love for the reprobate is not the love of value; it is the love of pity for that which *could* have had value and has none. It is a love of compassion. It is a love of sorrow. It is a love of pathos. It is the same deep sense of compassion and pity we have when we see a scab-ridden derelict lying in the gutter. It is not a love that is incompatible with revulsion, but it is a genuine, well-meant, compassionate, sympathetic love nonetheless.

THE START

It turns out that the good news about salvation starts with the bad news about sin. As Jesus said, "It is not those who are healthy who need a physician, but those who are sick; I did not come to call the righteous, but sinners" (Mark 2:17 NASB). Paul knew that those who underestimate the enormity and gravity of human sinfulness—especially those who do not see their own depravity—cannot apply the only effective remedy to their problems.

There can be no salvation for those who aren't convinced of the seriousness of their sin. There can be no word of reconciliation for sinners who remain oblivious to their estrangement from God. True fear of God cannot grip those who are blind to the depth of their sinfulness. And no mercy is available for those who do not tremble at God's holy threats.

In other words, to attempt to eradicate the human conscience is one of the most spiritually destructive pursuits any individual or society can engage in. It results in God's wrath—not yet ultimate wrath (hell) or eschatological wrath (the Day of the Lord), but temporal wrath. That is, He removes restraining grace and turns a person or a society over to the cycle of sin without the mitigating deterrent of conscience. This is the very judgment Paul spoke of at Lystra, when he said that God "in the generations gone by . . . permitted all the nations to go their own ways" (Acts 14:16 NASB).

That is Paul's main point in Romans 1:18–32. There he describes the judgment of God that results in humanity's decline into wanton sin. Notice that the most dramatic feature of his narrative is not the ghastly sins he names—although he chronicles some pretty gross practices. But the singular feature that marks each step of mankind's descent under God's wrath involves the hardening and decimation of the conscience.

THE CONSCIENCE
EVIDENT WITHIN

Paul said God's wrath is revealed because people "suppress the truth in unrighteousness" (Romans 1:18). He is referring to sinners who have successfully hushed their own consciences. "The truth" they suppress is innately known truth about the character of God, a sense of good and bad, and a basic knowledge of right and wrong. These things are universally known to all, "evident within them; for God made it evident to them" (v. 19 NASB). In other words, God manifests Himself in the most basic sense within every human conscience.

That internal knowledge about God is further augmented by evidences of His power and deity in the natural order of creation—"His invisible attributes, His eternal power and divine nature, have been clearly seen, being understood through what has been made" (v. 20 NASB). The truth thus revealed is not cryptic or ambiguous—it is "clearly seen." Nor is it observable only by a few specially gifted souls. "The heavens are telling of the glory of God; and their expanse is declaring the work of His hands" (Psalm 19:1 NASB). They testify to a universal audience.

In other words, these truths—that God exists, that He is powerful, that He is good, and that He is glorious—are evident to believers and non-believers, Christians and pagans, Jews and Gentiles. No one can plead ignorance. Even the most unenlightened pagan knows more truth than he is willing to accept. Those who suppress that truth—those who abrogate their consciences—"are without excuse" (Romans 1:20).

THE DOWNWARD SPIRAL

Paul traces the wrath of God through humanity's descent into deeper and more pervasive sin. He outlines the steps of that descent, and they read as if they had been taken from the front pages of our newspapers. The more modern society reaches into the abyss of unbelief and wantonness, the more the truth of Scripture is fulfilled. Notice how the issues Paul outlined nearly two thousand years ago describe precisely the sins most popular today. They appear in the following areas: secularism, lack of common sense, corrupt religion, uncontrolled lust, and sexual perversion.

The hard truth is that we humans are totally unable to live right and to please God on our own. We're lost without Him.

CONFESSION OF SIN

Your inability to obey God the way you know you should has an impact on your relationship with Him. Just as a disobedient child disappoints his father, so our sin disappoints our heavenly Father. Yet just as a father welcomes with open arms a child who confesses his disobedience with a repentant spirit, so God restores to us the joy of salvation when we confess our sin to Him (Psalm 51:12).

As part of your new life in Christ, you'll want to maintain that intimate relationship with Him. To do that you need to continually confess your sins to God. As the apostle John explained, "If we confess our sins, He is faithful and just to forgive us our sins and to cleanse us from all unrighteousness" (1 John 1:9). A Christian continually confesses and God continually forgives.

Scripture teaches that redeemed people are to pray regularly for forgiveness. As long as we live in a sinful world and have our own sinful tendencies, there is a sense in which we as Christians, though eternally cleansed, still need daily cleansing from the effects of sin.

You need to forsake your sin regularly, seeking not the pardon of an angry Judge but the forgiveness of your loving Father—displeased and grieved, yet loving all the same.

True confession of sin is not just admitting you did something wrong, but acknowledging that your sin was against God and in defiance of Him personally. Therefore the primary feature of confession is agreeing with God that you are helplessly guilty. In fact, the Greek word for confession literally means "say the same." To confess your sins is to say the same thing God says about them, acknowledging that God's perspective of your transgressions is correct.

For that reason, true confession also involves repentance—turning away from the evil thought or action. You have not honestly confessed your sins until you have expressed the desire to turn from them. Real confession includes a brokenness that inevitably leads to a change of behavior. In Isaiah 66:2, the Lord says, "On this one will I look: on him who is poor and of a contrite spirit, and who trembles at My word." When you pray, go to God trembling at breaking His Word, longing for victory over your weaknesses and failures. Confessing your sin, however, does not eliminate God's chastening (disciplining) work in your life. Though you repent, God will often chasten you to correct your behavior in the future. If He chastens you because of sinful behavior, you know you deserve the correction.

When God chastens us as His children, it is for our benefit. Hebrews 12:5–11 says He chastens us as sons so that we might be better sons. Too often believers have the wrong perspective on chastening, wondering why God would allow horrible things to happen to them. Confession allows us to view chastening from God's perspective. Only then can you see how God, through painful results, is shaping you by drawing you away from sin to righteousness.

Yet our God is a forgiving God. In response and thanks, we confess our sin to Him and turn from it, lest we trample on His grace. If you try to cover your sin, you will not prosper; you will only forfeit your joy and reap divine displeasure. But when you confess and forsake your sin, there is a guarantee of divine compassion. As wise King Solomon promised in Proverbs 28:13, "He who covers his sins will not prosper, but whoever confesses and forsakes them will have mercy." The God who disciplines sinning saints because of His love for them also delights to shower the brokenhearted and repentant with His mercy.

Sin is a reality of life on earth, but for Christians it is only a temporary, nagging nemesis. A glorious salvation awaits, by the grace of a loving Father who is ready to embrace you forever into His presence, having made you sinless at home in heaven.

CHAPTER 4

GOD WANTS
TO FORGIVE

THE PRODIGAL SON

"When he was still a great way off, his father saw him and had compassion, and ran and fell on his neck and kissed him" (Luke 15:20).

As Jesus was telling this story, the scribes and Pharisees surely expected the prodigal son's father to drop the hammer hard on the wayward youth. After all, the father's honor had been turned to shame by his son's rebellion, and the father had further brought shame on himself by the lenient way he responded to the boy at the start. Hopefully this father had learned a lesson even more valuable than whatever practical wisdom the prodigal had gained from his experiences. Any father with a proper concern about the honor of his own name and the reputation of the family would now see to it that a boy like this received the full and just deserts of all his transgressions, right?

Bear in mind that Jesus was telling this parable chiefly for the benefit of the scribes and Pharisees. In a story filled with shame and shock and surprises, they were nevertheless on board with Him up to this point.

Oh yes—they were greatly amazed and even skeptical at the part about the prodigal's repentance. But they definitely would affirm the boy's planned course of action: going home, humbling himself, confessing that he had been wrong, renouncing all rights to his position as a son, and working as a hired servant in an outcast's role while he labored to make restitution. All of that, by their way of thinking, was exactly what the wayward youth needed to do. Finally, some sanity in this story!

The Pharisees' Perspective

The gross improprieties of the prodigal son's early behavior remained a large, almost impassible obstacle, preventing the Pharisees from showing him any empathy or compassion. They simply couldn't hear about such shameful behavior without being demonstratively and permanently offended. Their worldview demanded it. The very thought of that kind of sin was so utterly distasteful to them that for all practical purposes, they treated it as unforgivable. Their carefully maintained public veneer was, after all, designed to show contempt for everything embodied in the prodigal's self-defilement: rebellion, worldliness, and other overt forms of conspicuous misbehavior. For them, when someone like that expressed any kind of repentance, even that was an occasion for scorn. They certainly had no category in their theology for showing grace to such a sinner.

So now that the boy was coming home, the Pharisees expected him to get what he deserved. The only question was how and how much the father would punish the boy—to save his own honor, and to shame the son in the way he deserved. Here was the part of the story that most captivated and appealed to their legalistic minds. By now they were engrossed.

One thing they were certain of: there could be no instant forgiveness. Nor was the prodigal likely to merit full reconciliation with his father, ever. If the rebel wanted to come back home now, he would simply have to take his medicine in full doses.

In the Pharisees' idea of a best-case scenario, the chastened son would be excluded from fellowship in his family. He would probably live as a pariah on the outskirts of his father's estate, shouldering the futile burden of trying to repay his debt to the father for the rest of his life. That, after all, was merciful in the extreme—especially compared to what justice demanded (Deuteronomy 28:18–21).

Under such an arrangement, the boy could earn a decent salary and even have a permanent place to live in the servants' quarters—job security and a livable wage. He would no longer face the daily threat of starvation. But that was it. He would enjoy no special privileges. Not only could he never be a son again, but he would have no status at all.

Why should he? He was the one who had renounced his own heritage and chose to live like a Gentile. In doing that, he forfeited forever all the rights that were his in his father's household. He could have no further share in his father's estate. After all, he had already received his full inheritance, liquidated it for much less than its value, and squandered it away. If the father followed social conventions, he already would have punctuated the prodigal's renunciation of his own family with finality by having a funeral for the boy shortly after he had left home.

So as far as the Pharisees were concerned, the prodigal was already dead to his father. He could consider himself fortunate indeed if the father even agreed to his request that he hire him as a common laborer. That was all mercy demanded, and it was the best option the penitent son could ever hope for. But he would still have to do a lifetime of hard labor in a hired servant's role. That's just how such things were supposed to be handled.

So what happened next was a seismic jolt to the Pharisees' worldview. Their eyes would roll and their heads would shake with shock and outrage at the reception the father gave the prodigal son.

What Everyone Expected

As the prodigal son approached his father's home, the reality and urgency of his situation must have been at the forefront of all his thinking. His life was now completely dependent on the mercy of his father. Without the father's resources, he would have no hope whatsoever. Everyone else in the village would certainly scorn him; people had to do that to protect their own honor. The prodigal therefore hung helpless in the balance between life and death, and if his father turned him away, he would be doomed. In that culture, no one would even think of taking him in if his own father declared him an outcast. So everything hinged on his father's response.

As he drew nearer to his home, the prodigal must have rehearsed his plea dozens, maybe hundreds, of times: "Father, I have sinned against heaven and before you, and I am no longer worthy to be called your son. Make me like one of your hired servants" (Luke 15:18–19).

Perhaps he wondered how that request would sound to reasonable minds. Was it outrageous for him to seek his father's mercy? Was he asking too much to ask for any favor at all? That's how the typical person in that culture might feel. That's certainly how the Pharisees saw it. The prodigal's conscience would be scourging him with reminders of all the foolish and wicked things he had done that dishonored his father. Who was he to ask for help now—especially since he had already been given so much and squandered it all and thus had nothing left of any real value to offer in return for his father's kindness? What if the father took his plea for mercy as just another scandalous request and turned him away forever?

In that culture of honor, especially in a situation like this, it would be nothing extraordinary if the father simply refused to meet the boy face-to-face. In fact, even if the father were inclined to grant the penitent son an audience, it would be fairly typical to punish him first by making a public spectacle of his shame. For example, a father in those circumstances might have the son sit outside the gate in public view for several days, letting him soak up some of the dishonor he had brought upon his own family. The boy would be completely exposed to the elements—and worse, to the utter derision of the whole community.

You see, in a typical village where everyone knew everyone else, the significance of such a gesture from the father would be instantly understood by all. If a father denied his own son an immediate face-to-face meeting and made him sit in the public square instead, the entire village would treat the boy with utter scorn—mocking and verbally abusing him and possibly even spitting on him. Less privileged people in the community would go out of their way to show their disdain for this boy who had been blessed with every advantage and had thrown it all away. No indignity would be too great to heap on his head. He would just have to sit there and take it while he waited.

That may seem harsh, but remember—the full penalty prescribed by Moses' law for such a rebellious son was death by public stoning. The instructions in the Law ordered that "all the men of his city shall stone him to death with stones; so you shall put away the evil from among you" (Deuteronomy 21:21). So public humiliation in lieu of stoning was actually a mercy the boy did not deserve. And in that culture where honor and shame meant so much, the community's profound contempt for this boy's behavior practically demanded some kind of expression.

Most likely, that's precisely the kind of treatment the prodigal son expected. It was the cost of readmission to the village he himself had shunned. It was just one phase of a long process he would need to be prepared to endure. If the prodigal had counted the cost of repentance, such treatment should not even take him by surprise. By the social customs of that culture, having been the cause of so much shame, he now needed to be shamed by everyone else, as a vital part of the just retribution he deserved. He had made himself a pariah; he'd have to expect to be treated like one.

After a few days' wait like that, if the father did decide to grant him an audience—assuming he was willing to extend a measure of mercy to the penitent rebel—the son would be expected to bow low and kiss the father's feet. No embrace. It would not even be right for him to stand and kiss his father's hand. The only proper demeanor for such a son would be to fall prostrate with his face to the ground before the father whom he had disgraced.

The father would most likely meet him with a measure of frigid indifference. To save face, the father would need to approach the arrangement formally, like a business deal, without showing any overt affection or tenderness for the boy. There was no negotiation to be done; the father would simply outline the terms of employment—spelling out what would be required of the boy, what kind of labor he could expect to be assigned, and how long he needed to serve before he could be given even the smallest measure of privilege.

AN OLD TESTAMENT PARALLEL: JOSEPH AND HIS BROTHERS

We see an interesting parallel to this situation in the Old Testament account of Joseph's reconciliation with his brothers. The story should be familiar to most—how the brothers sold Joseph into slavery, and yet he famously rose despite every conceivable trial and setback to become the second most powerful man in Egypt.

Years later, when the brothers were forced by a famine to go into Egypt to seek relief, they encountered Joseph without realizing who he was. At first (until he learned from them the whereabouts of their father and youngest brother), Joseph used a stern, even threatening, demeanor with them. He had no intention of harming them, of course. But to elicit their cooperation and complete honesty—and perhaps to discover whether they were the least bit remorseful for their sin against him—Joseph used his authority to good advantage. He made his brothers sweat (over a period of several days or weeks, it seems) until he was ready to reveal who he was and assure his brothers of his forgiveness.

Of course, Joseph had no duty to show his brothers that kind of favor, and he had every right to punish them for what they had done to him. They knew it too. Even after Joseph revealed his true identity and welcomed them with tears, they still feared what he might do. When their father, Jacob, died, they thought Joseph might decide to seek revenge. So they offered to be made his servants (Genesis 50:18). Joseph then made it absolutely clear that he forgave them completely and unconditionally.

But Joseph's forgiveness toward his brothers was an extraordinary, otherworldly, one-of-a-kind act from one of the most renowned figures in Israel's history. No one would expect anything like that from the prodigal's father—not the prodigal son himself, not the villagers in his father's community, not his elder brother, not the people in Jesus' audience, and certainly not the Pharisees.

CHAPTER 5

GOD ACTS TO FORGIVE

HOW THE PLOT SHIFTED

At this point, Jesus' parable suddenly took another dramatic and unexpected turn. Here was a father not merely willing to grant a measure of mercy in return for the promise of a lifetime of meritorious service—but eager to forgive freely, completely, at the very first sign of repentance: "When he was still a great way off, his father saw him and had compassion, and ran and fell on his neck and kissed him" (Luke 15:20).

It is evident that the father was looking diligently for the prodigal's return. How else could he have seen him while he was still a long way off? We can safely imagine that the father had been looking steadily, scanning the horizon daily, repeatedly, for signs of the boy's return. He had been at it a long time too—probably since long before the initial shock of the boy's departure had even worn off.

Obviously, the heartache had not yet worn off, because the father was still watching. And he kept watching daily, heartbroken but hopeful, privately bearing the unspeakable pain of suffering love for his son. He surely knew that the kind of life his son was headed for would eventually end up the way it did. He desperately hoped the boy would survive and come back home. So he filled his spare time watching expectantly. He must have gone to the highest point on his property—perhaps on a tower or rooftop—and spent his idle moments scanning the horizon, praying for the boy's safe return, and thinking about what it would be like when and if the prodigal returned. A man such as this father would probably have turned that scenario over in his own mind countless times.

It was daylight when the father finally spotted the wayward boy. (We know that detail because it's the only way he could have seen him "a great way off.") That meant the village center was full of people. The markets were busy with merchants selling, people buying, women with children, and older people sitting in the public square while they watched the bustling activity. The moment the son approached the village, someone would no doubt recognize him and shout the news of his return. Someone else would likely run to tell the father about it.

So why was the father watching? And why did he run to the son rather than waiting for the son to come to him? First, and most obviously, the father was truly eager to initiate forgiveness and reconciliation with his son. That aspect of this parable echoes the previous two parables, where the shepherd diligently sought his lost sheep and the woman feverishly searched for her lost coin. Each of those images pictures Christ as the faithful Seeker. He is the architect and the initiator of our salvation. He seeks and draws sinners to Himself before they ever would think of seeking Him. He always makes the first overture. He Himself pays the redemption-price. He calls, justifies, sanctifies, and finally glorifies each believing sinner (Romans 8:30). Every aspect of our salvation is His gracious work.

This imagery of the father running to meet the prodigal son fills in the details of the big picture even more. It illustrates the truth that God is slow to anger and swift to forgive. He has no pleasure in the death of the wicked but is eager, willing, even delighted to save sinners.

WHAT WAS THE
FATHER THINKING?

There's a second major factor at play here, however. The father clearly wanted to reach the prodigal before the boy reached the village—apparently to protect him from the outpouring of scorn and invective he would surely receive if he walked through that village unreconciled with his father. The father himself would bear the shame and take the abuse instead.

And make no mistake: in the context of that culture, the father's action of running to the boy and embracing him before he even came all the way home was seen as a shameful breech of decorum. In the jaded perspective of the scribes and Pharisees, this was just one more thing that added to the father's shame. For one thing, noblemen in that culture did not run. Running was for little boys and servants. Grown men did not run—especially men of dignity and importance. They walked magisterially, with a slow gait and deliberate steps.

But Jesus said "his father . . . *ran*" (Luke 15:20, emphasis added). He did not send a servant or a messenger ahead to intercept his son. And it was not merely that he quickened his pace. He ran. The text uses a word that speaks of sprinting, as if he were in an athletic competition. The father gathered up the hem of his robe and took off in a most undignified manner.

The image of a respectable, wealthy, honorable man such as this running seems so out of place in Middle Eastern culture that Arabic Bible translators have traditionally been reluctant to translate the phrase without resorting to a euphemism such as "he hurried," or "he presented himself." Kenneth E. Bailey, an evangelical Bible commentator who lived in the Middle East and made careful studies of the language and culture there, wrote:

The reluctance on the part of the Arabic versions to let the father run is amazing. . . . For a thousand years a wide range of such phrases were employed (almost as if there was a conspiracy) to avoid the humiliating truth of the text—the father ran! The explanation for all of this is simple. The tradition identified the father with God, and running in public is too humiliating to attribute to a person who symbolizes God. Not until 1860, with the appearance of the Bustani–Van Dyck Arabic Bible, does the father appear running. The work sheets of the translators are available to me and even in that great version the first rendition of the Greek was "he hurried," and only in the second round of the translation process does rakada (he ran) appear. The Hebrew of Prov. 19:2 reads, "He that hastens with his feet sins" (my translation). The father represents God. How could he run? He does.[1]

The father was humbling himself, even though the prodigal son was the one who should have been doing so.

Most of us today would see this moment when the father ran to embrace his son as the most poignant, tender moment in the parable. It was certainly not viewed that way by the Pharisees. Nor would the typical listener in Jesus' audience simply take it in stride and admire the father's compassion. This was a scandal. It was shocking. It was even more offensive to them than the sins of the prodigal.

But the father was nevertheless willing to have the villagers whisper among themselves, "What does he think he is doing? This boy took advantage of his father and sinned horribly against him. The boy should be made an outcast. Instead, this man who was dishonored by his own son now dishonors himself even more by embracing the wretched boy!" The father in effect positioned himself between his son and all the scorn, taunting, and abuse people in that culture would naturally have heaped on the boy's head.

Our version says the father "had compassion" (Luke 5:20), but the Greek expression is even more emphatic. It uses a word that literally speaks of a sensation in the viscera—or in today's vernacular, a gut feeling. The father was powerfully moved with compassion, an emotion so deep and so forceful that it made his stomach churn.

The father's compassion was not merely sorrow over his son's past sin. Nor was it only a momentary sympathy prompted by the boy's present filthiness. (Remember, the prodigal was by now in rags and smelled like pigs.) Certainly the father's feeling toward the son included a deep sense of pity over all the terrible things sin had already done to him. But it seems obvious that something else was amplifying the father's anguish at that precise moment.

His action of running toward the son and intercepting him on the road suggests he had something terribly urgent and immediate on his mind. That's why I am convinced that what moved the father to run was a deep sense of empathy in anticipation of the contempt that was sure to be poured on the son as he walked through the village. The father took off in a sprint in order to be the first person to reach him, so that he could deflect the abuse he knew the boy would suffer.

This is indeed a fitting picture of Christ, who humbled Himself to seek and to save the lost—and then "endured the cross, despising the shame" (Hebrews 12:2). Like this father, He willingly took upon Himself all the bitter scorn, the contempt, the mockery, and the wrath our sin fully deserves. He even took our guilt upon His own innocent shoulders. He bore everything for our sake and in our stead.

If the truth were known, this father's behavior, undignified as it might have seemed to Jesus' audience, was actually nothing very remarkable compared to the amazing grace unveiled in the incarnation and death of Christ. As a matter of fact, that was one of the key lessons Jesus was challenging the Pharisees with through His tale.

AN AMAZING DISPLAY OF GRACE

When the father reached the wayward son, he couldn't contain his affection, and he didn't hesitate in granting forgiveness. This was even more shocking to the Pharisees than the imagery of a grown man sprinting down a dusty road to greet a derelict son.

The father immediately embraced the prodigal. Jesus said the father "fell on his neck and kissed him" (Luke 5:20). The verb tense means he kissed him repeatedly. He collapsed on the boy in a massive hug, buried his head in the neck of his son—stinking and dirty and unpresentable as he was—and welcomed him with a display of unbridled emotion.

It is evident that the father had been suffering in quiet grief the entire time the boy was gone. His deep love for the youth had never once wavered. The yearning to see him wise up and come home must have been a painful burning in the father's heart. It filled his thoughts every day. And now that he saw the bedraggled figure of his son alone on the horizon, it mattered little to the father what people thought of him; he was determined to welcome home the boy as personally and publicly as possible.

Furthermore, the father would spare the boy from any more of the reproach of his sin—by becoming a reproach himself. In essence, he took the boy's disgrace completely upon himself—emptying himself of all pride, renouncing his fatherly rights, not caring at all about his own honor (even in that culture, where honor seemed like everything). And in an amazing display of selfless love—openly despising the shame of it all (Hebrews 12:2)—he opened his arms to the returning sinner and hugged him tightly in an embrace designed partly to shield him from any more humiliation. By the time the boy walked into the village, he was already fully reconciled to his father.

The prodigal had come home prepared to kiss his father's feet. Instead, the father was kissing the prodigal's pig-stinking head. Such an embrace with repeated kisses was a gesture that signified not only the father's delirious joy but also his full acceptance, friendship, love, forgiveness, restoration, and total reconciliation. It was a deliberate and demonstrative way of signaling to the whole village that the father had fully forgiven his son, without any qualms or hesitancy.

What a beautiful picture this is of the forgiveness offered in the gospel! The typical sinner wants out of the morass of sin, and his first instinct is to devise a plan. He will work off his guilt. He will reform himself. But such a plan could never succeed. The debt is too great to repay, and the sinner is helpless to change his own status. He is fallen, and he cannot alter that fact. So the Savior intercepts him. Christ has already run the gauntlet, taken the shame for Himself, suffered the rebukes, borne the cruel taunts, and paid the price of the guilt in full. He embraces the sinner, pours out love upon him, grants complete forgiveness, and reconciles him to God.

A SPEECH INTERRUPTED

It is significant that the father was already granting forgiveness before the son said a word. After the father embraced him, the prodigal started to make the confession he had been rehearsing: "Father, I have sinned against heaven and in your sight, and am no longer worthy to be called your son" (Luke 15:21)—but he barely got that far and the father quickly cut him off, giving orders to the servants to begin preparations for a celebratory banquet.

The prodigal never even got to the part of his rehearsed speech in which he would ask to become one of the hired servants. By the time he completed his first sentence, the father had already reinstated him as a beloved son, and the great celebration was under way.

The father seems to have perceived the depth and reality of the boy's repentance from the simple fact that the boy had come home. He knew his own son well enough to know what his return signified. He could tell from the boy's appalling condition how much he had suffered the cruel consequences of his sin. So he didn't even permit the boy to finish making his confession before he granted him mercy. This was an act of grace that went far, far beyond anything the boy had ever dared to hope for.

The prodigal's unfinished confession may seem a subtle detail in the parable, but it made a not-so-subtle point for the Pharisees' benefit. There was no way they could have failed to notice one glaring reality in Jesus' description of the father's eagerness to forgive. The boy had done nothing whatsoever to atone for his own sin, and yet the father's forgiveness was full and lavish anyway, with nothing held back.

As far as the Pharisees were concerned, this outpouring of love and forgiveness toward a flagrant and self-confessed sinner was radical and totally unorthodox. Doesn't common sense demand that sins be atoned for? Didn't God Himself say He will not justify the wicked (Exodus 23:7) and that He will by no means allow the guilty to go unpunished (Exodus 34:7)? How could a notorious rebel like the prodigal son simply be let off scot-free? Whatever happened to righteousness? What about the principles of divine justice? Wasn't the entire Old Testament system filled to overflowing with priests and sacrifices and other symbols of atonement—precisely in order to stress this fundamental truth?

But our God acts to forgive; He runs to the prodigal, to us.

CHAPTER 6

GOD PROVIDES THE WAY TO FORGIVENESS

THE NECESSITY OF ATONEMENT

It is quite true that sin must be atoned for. Don't imagine for a moment that when God forgives sin, He simply looks the other way and pretends the sin never occurred. Moses' law was filled with bloody sacrifices precisely to make that truth inescapable.

This point is crucial and ultimately pivotal in understanding the parable of the prodigal son. Remember that the main point Jesus was making in this parable was for the Pharisees' benefit. He was addressing their faulty idea about God—that He found joy in their self-righteousness rather than in the forgiveness of sins. Their theology was so lacking any sense of true grace that they simply could not account for how forgiven sinners might stand before God apart from a lifetime of religious effort. The Pharisees' misunderstanding about what is required to make full atonement for sin lay at the root of their errant theology.

Don't forget how the Pharisees had overlaid the truth of the Old Testament with their own elaborate system of human traditions, man-made rules, and useless ceremonies. They were convinced sinners needed to do good works to help atone for their own sins. They had even enshrined their own intricate system of finely detailed traditions as the chief means by which they thought it possible to acquire the kind of merit they believed would balance out the guilt of sin. That is why they were obsessed with ostentatious works, religious rituals, spiritual stunts, ceremonial displays of righteousness, and other external and cosmetic achievements. And they clung doggedly to that system, even though most of their rituals were nothing more than their own inventions, designed to paper over sin and make them appear righteous.

Here was the problem with that: even authentically good works could never accomplish what the Pharisees hoped their ceremonial traditions would accomplish. That was made perfectly clear by the Law itself. The Law demanded no less than absolute perfection (Matthew 5:19, 48; James 2:10). And it was filled from start to finish with threats and curses against anyone who violated it at any point. The reason we need atonement is that we are fallen sinners who cannot keep the Law adequately. Why would anyone ever think to earn enough merit to atone for sin through an imperfect obedience to the Law? That was the fatal flaw in the Pharisees' system.

In fact, the Law itself made perfectly clear that the price of full atonement was more costly than any mere human could ever possibly pay: "The soul who sins shall die" (Ezekiel 18:4).

Notice that Jesus did not mention anything about the actual means of atonement in the parable of the prodigal son. That, after all, wasn't the point of the story. But our Lord did nevertheless directly confront the heart of the Pharisees' error, which was their insistence that all sinners need to perform certain works to atone for their own sin—and thus earn the forgiveness and favor of God.

THE ONLY WAY TO BE JUSTIFIED BEFORE GOD

The parable of the prodigal son debunks that false idea. It illustrates instead the simple truth of how and why repentant faith is the only means by which any sinner can find justification before God. Forgiveness is not a reward for merits we earn by good works. Don't imagine, however, that practical righteousness is eliminated altogether—because good works are the inevitable fruit of faith. But sinners who repent and turn to God are fully and instantly justified, freely forgiven from the first moment of faith's inception—before a single good work is done.

That was the principal lesson of Abraham's example. "He *believed in the LORD*, and He accounted it to him for righteousness" (Genesis 15:6, emphasis added). His faith was the sole means by which he laid hold of God's promises. In Romans 4, Paul makes an extended argument showing that David was likewise justified though faith alone, rather than through the performance of any good deeds, religious rituals, or meritorious works designed to nullify the debt of sin.

In a similar way, the prodigal son is a textbook example of someone who is justified by grace through faith apart from meritorious deeds. His forgiveness was a fully settled reality, and his status as a privileged son was established beyond question before he ever even had an opportunity to finish expressing his repentance.

That lifetime of work he was prepared to offer as a servant to his father? It was utterly unnecessary as a means of earning the father's favor. The father had granted his full blessing and unconditional pardon by grace alone.

But this repentant young man would nevertheless be permanently changed because of the grace his father showed him. Why would he ever go back to a life of self-indulgence and prodigality? He had already pursued sin to its inevitable end and knew the results all too well. He was severely chastened by the bitterness of that experience. He had drunk the awful dregs of sin's consequences.

But now the blinders had been taken from his eyes. He saw his father in a new light, and he loved him with a new appreciation. He had every reason henceforth to remain faithful. He would be serving his father now with gladness—not as a hired servant but with the full status of a beloved son.

THE NARROW WAY AND A BOGUS INVITATION

I know this shocks some people, because we hear all the time that getting saved is easy. "Just sign this little card!" "Just raise your hand!" "Just walk down that aisle while the choir sings one more stanza!" "Just recite this prayer." "Just ask Jesus into your heart." It all sounds simple. The only problem is that none of those actions has anything to do with real salvation and getting through the narrow gate. That sort of invitationalism implies that Jesus is some poor pitiful Savior, waiting for us to make the first move to allow Him His way. It implies that salvation hinges on a human decision, as if the power that saves us were the power of human "free will."

This emphasis is a peculiarly American phenomenon that started in the nineteenth century with a New York lawyer-turned-evangelist named Charles Finney. He was the most formidable American anti-Calvinist, and he insisted that people get saved by an act of sheer willpower. Therefore, whatever is necessary in order to manipulate their wills is an essential method, because whatever it takes to convince them to decide to be saved is legitimate. The end justifies the means. And so the manipulative "altar call" became a major focus of his evangelism. Up to that time, American evangelists were, for the most part, Calvinistic, that is, they believed that sinners are saved by hearing the message of the gospel while God the Holy Spirit awakens them from sinful deadness.

But Finney took a different path. He made emotional appeals and taught that salvation required no sovereign regeneration by God, but only the act of the human will. The people came streaming down the aisle under the force of his cleverness. The vast majority of these weren't real conversions; in fact, Finney later admitted that his ministry had produced mostly halfhearted and temporary "converts." But the spectacle of crowds surging forward was very convincing.

Dwight L. Moody picked up the technique from Finney, and he passed it along to a generation of stadium evangelists and ministry leaders who still stage sometimes enormous public events and manipulate people to come to the stage. Most of that activity is fruitless. No doubt I believe that, in spite of the manipulation and not because of it, some of the people who take a pledge, sign a card, or come down front at those services are brokenhearted, aware of their sinfulness, and ready to follow Jesus as Lord by bearing their crosses with total self-denial. Those are the people who will be taken in at the narrow gate by the power of God through the truth, who will find themselves on the highway to heaven. The rest will not, but may be deceived.

According to Jesus, it's very, very difficult to be saved. At the end of Matthew 7:14, He said of the narrow gate, "There are few who find it." I don't believe anyone ever slipped and fell into the kingdom of God. That's cheap grace, easy-believism, Christianity Lite, a shallow, emotional revivalist approach: "I believe in Jesus!" "Fine, you're part of the family, come on in!" No. The few who find the narrow gate have to search hard for it, then come through it alone. It's hard to find a church or preacher—or a Christian—who can direct you to it.

The kingdom is for those who agonize to enter it, whose hearts are shattered over their sinfulness, who mourn in meekness, who hunger and thirst and long for God to change their lives. It's hard because you've got all hell against you. One of Satan's pervasive lies in the world today is that it's easy to become a Christian. It's not easy at all. It's a very narrow gate that you must find and go through alone, anguished over your sinfulness and longing for forgiveness.

Somebody might say this sounds like the religion of human achievement. Not so. When you come to brokenness, the recognition that you, of yourself, cannot make it through the narrow gate, then Christ pours into you grace upon grace to strengthen you for that entrance. In your brokenness, His power becomes your resource. Our part is to admit our sin and inability and plead for mercy and power from on high.

NO BAGGAGE

You can't go through a turnstile with baggage. To get through the narrow gate that leads to heaven, you leave all your possessions behind and enter empty-handed. It's not the gate of the self-contented, who want to carry all their stuff in with them; it's the gate of the self-denying, who strip off all self-righteousness and self-reliance. Rejecting all they have been, they leave their former lives behind. Otherwise, they can't get through the gate. Nor can anybody else.

The rich young ruler made it to the gate and asked Jesus what he had to do to enter the kingdom. The Lord told him to drop his matched set of Gucci luggage and come on through. He had found the gate that few people ever find, but he refused to enter because he was too selfish and self-centered to make the sacrifice Jesus asked of him.

The point here is wonderfully expressed in Matthew 18:3, where Jesus says, "Unless you are converted and become as little children, you will by no means enter the kingdom of heaven." The distinctive mark of children is that they are utterly dependent on others and have achieved nothing of merit themselves. As the hymn writer puts it, "Nothing in my hand I bring, simply to Thy cross I cling." Saving faith is more than an act of the mind; it is a disdain for one's sinful self, an admission of unworthiness, a naked plea: "Lord, be merciful to me, a sinner!"

There's nothing wrong with raising our hands or saying a little prayer, but those things do not bring true salvation apart from authentic faith in Christ. Jesus called for a narrow, difficult, radical, dramatic admission of sinfulness; an acknowledgment that we are nothing and have nothing with which to commend ourselves to God. Faith begins when we throw ourselves on His mercy for forgiveness.

REPENTANCE AND SURRENDER

To come through the narrow gate, you must enter with your heart repentant over sin, ready to turn from loving sin to loving the Lord. When John the Baptist was preparing a people to receive the Messiah, they were coming to be baptized because they wanted to have their sins forgiven. To any Jew, preparation for the coming of the Messiah and readiness for His kingdom meant purging the heart of its sinfulness.

You must also enter the narrow gate in utter surrender to Christ. No one can be regenerate, as Christ indicates in Matthew 7, by simply adding Jesus Christ to his carnal activities. Salvation is not an addition; it's a transformation that leads to willing submission to His Word. The whole message of 1 John is that if you are truly redeemed, it will manifest itself in a transformed life in which you confess sin, characteristically obey the Lord, and manifest love for the Lord and others. The divine miracle of a changed life reveals true salvation, resulting in a heart that desires to obey the Lord. As Jesus said, "If you abide in My word, you are My disciples indeed" (John 8:31).

If someone who calls himself a Christian doesn't think and act like a Christian, he's not on the road he thinks he is. He has likely joined the mighty band rushing through the wide gate of false religion. He exhibits none of this self-denial stuff: "Hey, bring all your baggage, your personal ambition, your will, your selfish desires, your immorality, your lack of repentance, your reluctance even to submit fully to the leadership of Christ! You can just come right on through the gate of self-indulgence!" Many claim to be Christians and yet are totally self-indulgent. They will never get through the narrow gate with all that baggage. Though they may not know it, they are on the broad road to destruction.

STANDING AT THE CROSSROADS

Once you've come in the wide gate, the whole gang's there and life is easy: no rules, no rigid morality, and plenty of tolerance and diversity just as long as you say you love Jesus. All the desires of the fallen heart are fed on that road. There's no need for humility, or to study the Word of God. It takes absolutely no effort; as with a dead fish floating downstream, the current does it all. It's what Ephesians 2:2 describes as "the course of this world." It's the broad road where "the way of the ungodly shall perish" (Psalm 1:6).

Contrast this with the narrow way. The best translation of the text in Matthew 7:13–14 would be a "constricted" way. It literally means to press together or be confined, as in a narrow place on a precipice. That's why Paul said in Ephesians that we must walk circumspectly, with our eyes open, and not wander around. It's a very restricted way, hemmed in on both sides by the chastening hand of God. You step off this side and—*whack*—you get your spiritual knuckles hit! Same on the other side. The requirements are firm, strict, refined, and clear-cut, and there's no room for any deviation or departure from them. It must be the desire of our hearts to fulfill them, knowing full well that when we fail, God will chasten, and then God will wonderfully and lovingly forgive and set us on our feet again to pursue His will.

The choice, then, is between these two destinations: the broad way that leads to destruction, and the narrow way that is the only highway to heaven. All forms of the religion of human achievement—from humanism and atheism (the ultimate religion of human achievement, where man himself is God) to pseudo-Christianity—are going to end up in the same hell. As John Bunyan said, "For some the entrance to hell is from the portals of heaven." What a shock it's going to be for some people. The narrow way is going to open up into eternal bliss. On the other hand the broad way narrows down into a terrible pit. The narrow way widens into the endless glories of heaven, the fullness of an unspeakable, everlasting, unclouded fellowship of joy with God that we can't even imagine.

In Matthew 10:32–33, Jesus said, "Therefore whoever confesses Me before men, him I will also confess before My Father who is in heaven. But whoever denies Me before men, him I will also deny before My Father who is in heaven." Are you willing to confess the Christ of the New Testament, who is the true Christ, and the gospel He proclaimed, which is the true gospel? Are you unashamed, so that you will openly and publicly confess them? Or are you ashamed of Him and His words, and consequently you deny that He is who He says He is or that His gospel is the true message? If you are a denier, if you are ashamed of Him, if the preaching of the cross is, to you, foolish, then you are among the perishing.

Admiration is not enough. Saying you appreciate Christ and you serve Christ are not enough. Many on the broad road are those who have admired Jesus, but they didn't come through the narrow gate. They didn't come with broken and contrite hearts. They didn't come crushed under the weight of the law of God with a penitent attitude, embracing their true condition as desperate and damned, and crying out for salvation from the only source: the Lord Jesus Christ.

CHAPTER 7

GOD WANTS US TO FORGIVE OTHERS

JESUS CAME TO FORGIVE SINNERS

We know Matthew as the writer of the gospel that bears his name. But he was an unlikely disciple. In fact, everything about Matthew would have been odious to faithful Israelites. Publicans were the lowest and most despised of all the social outcasts in all the land. They were considered the most despicable of sinners, and they often lived up to that reputation in every conceivable sense. Pharisees and common people alike viewed them with the utmost scorn.

A SHORT TIME LINE

Not only do all three Synoptic Gospels place the call of Matthew immediately after the healing of the paralytic (Luke 5); both Matthew and Luke indicate that what follows happened immediately, on that same day. "As Jesus passed on from there, He saw a man named Matthew sitting at the tax office" (Matthew 9:9). "After these things He went out and saw a tax collector named Levi, sitting at the tax office" (Luke 5:27). Apparently, as soon as the paralyzed man picked up his pallet and left for home, Jesus went out of the house where the healing had taken place and started toward the lakeshore. In a village as small as Capernaum, situated right at water's edge, that could not be more than a few blocks.

Mark indicated that Jesus' plan was to continue teaching the multitudes, and the waterfront obviously afforded a better, more suitable venue than a house for that. As "He went out again by the sea" (Mark 2:13), somewhere along the way "He saw Levi the son of Alphaeus sitting at the tax office" (v. 14).

The tax office was obviously well situated so that Matthew could amass maximum revenue. Tradesmen trying to save time and bypass the hazardous Galilean road system regularly shipped goods by water across the Sea of Galilee. Capernaum was one of the best places on the north shore to connect with the Via Maris—a major thoroughfare between Damascus and the Mediterranean. Matthew was perfectly positioned at that unusual crossroads so that he could intercept and tax traffic in all directions, whether by water or by land. He could also keep an eye on the lucrative fishing trade in Capernaum and assess regular tariffs on the fishermen.

That means Matthew was perhaps the least likely person in all of Capernaum to become one of Jesus' twelve closest followers. The other disciples, mostly fishermen from Capernaum, undoubtedly knew him well, and they must have despised the way he had made himself wealthy off their livelihood.

"FOLLOW ME!"

But on that day, as Jesus passed the tax office, He caught Matthew's eye and gave him a simple two-word greeting: "Follow Me!" All three accounts of this incident record just that; no more. Matthew was obviously a man already under conviction. He had borne the weight of sin and guilt long enough, and upon hearing that simple command from Jesus, "he left all, rose up, and followed Him" (Luke 5:28).

For a man in Matthew's position, leaving everything behind so quickly was a dramatic turnaround comparable to the paralytic's sudden ability to walk and carry his own stretcher. Matthew's heart change was a spiritual rebirth, but no less miraculous than the paralytic's instant physical healing. As far as Matthew's career was concerned, this was a total and irreversible change of course. You could not walk away from a Roman tax commission and then have second thoughts and ask for your office back two days later. But Matthew did not hesitate: his sudden repentance is one of the most dramatic conversions described anywhere in Scripture.

In a village the size of Capernaum (fewer than two hundred yards from water's edge to the northern perimeter of the village), it is virtually certain that Matthew's office was very near the house where Jesus healed the paralytic. Given the commotion of the crowd, it would be impossible for the events of that day to escape Matthew's notice. He must have perked up when Jesus declared the paralytic man's sins forgiven. He was, after all, a publican and social outcast.

We can discern from his immediate response to Jesus that he was utterly fed up with the life of sin. He was probably feeling the spiritual barrenness that goes with ill-gotten material wealth. And it is clear that he was sensing the weight of his own guilt under the Holy Spirit's conviction. Jesus had just granted a forlorn quadriplegic the very thing Matthew's own soul craved: forgiveness, cleansing, and a pronouncement of justification. Coming from Someone like Jesus, who obviously had the authority to back up His decrees, that would definitely have caught Matthew's attention. Clearly, before Jesus even walked by and spoke to him, Matthew was being drawn to faith because of what he had seen that day.

Matthew's perspective was the polar opposite of the Pharisees'. He yearned to be free from his sin; they would not even admit that they were sinners. No wonder Matthew's response to Jesus was so immediate.

WHY DOES JESUS CONSORT WITH PUBLICANS AND SINNERS?

Matthew decided to host a celebratory reception for Jesus that very day. Like all new converts, he desperately wanted to introduce as many of his friends as possible to Jesus without delay. So he opened his home and invited Jesus as guest of honor. Luke says "a great number of tax collectors and others" came to the banquet (5:29). The "others" would of course be the kind of lowlifes who were willing to socialize with a group of publicans. In other words, this gathering would not have included any of the regulars from the local synagogue.

That a rabbi would be willing to fraternize at a party with such people was utterly repugnant to the Pharisees. It was diametrically opposed to all their doctrines about separation and ceremonial uncleanness. Here was yet another pet issue of the Pharisees, and Jesus was openly violating their standards, knowing full well that they were watching Him closely. From their perspective, it must have seemed as if He was deliberately flaunting His contempt for their system.

Because He was. Remember an important fact we stressed in the previous chapter: all the friction that has taken place out in the open thus far between Jesus and Israel's religious elite has been entirely at His instigation. As far as we know from Scripture, they had not yet voiced a single unprovoked criticism or public accusation against Him.

Even now, the Pharisees were not yet bold enough to complain to Jesus directly. They sought out His disciples and murmured their protest to them. Again, all three Synoptics stress that the Pharisees took their grievance to the disciples. It was a craven attempt to blindside Jesus by provoking a debate with His followers instead. I like the way Luke says it: "The Pharisees and their scribes began grumbling at His disciples" (5:30 NASB).

But Jesus overheard (Matthew 9:12; Mark 2:17), and He answered the Pharisees directly, with a single statement that became the definitive motto for His interaction with the self-righteous Sanhedrin and their ilk: "It is not those who are healthy who need a physician, but those who are sick; I did not come to call the righteous, but sinners" (Mark 2:17 NASB). For sinners and tax collectors seeking relief from the burden of their sin, Jesus had nothing but good news. To the self-righteous religious experts, He had nothing to say at all.

Harsh? By postmodern standards, this was a terribly strident thing to say. And (as many people today would quickly point out) there was virtually no possibility that a comment like this would help sway the Pharisees to Jesus' point of view. It was likelier to increase their hostility against Him.

And yet it was the right thing for Him to say at this moment. It was the truth they needed to hear. The fact that they were not "open" to it did not alter Jesus' commitment to speaking the truth—without toning it down, without bending it to fit His audience's tastes and preferences, without setting the facts of the gospel aside to speak to their "felt needs" instead.

The Pharisees evidently had no answer for Jesus. None of the gospels record anything further that they said. Here again, they simply lapse into silence and fade into the background of the narrative.

Their strategy when embarrassed like this seemed to be that they would fall back, regroup, rethink their strategy, and simply look for a different way to accuse Him. Each time, they would come back more determined and a little more bold.

Their attempts to discredit Jesus were by no means over. In fact, the Pharisees had only begun to fight.

Jesus was clear about His mission—He came for sinners, for us. And He wants us to reach out to the outcasts of the world, sharing the good news that their sins can be forgiven too.

THE DEPTH OF LOVE

We share the good news and we also live it, loving others and forgiving them. As Peter reminds us: "Above all things have fervent love for one another, for 'love will cover a multitude of sins'" (1 Peter 4:8).

Christians are to love to the limit, which involves covering a "multitude of sins." Sin must be dealt with but must also be forgiven. That's what "cover" implies. We are to put a blanket over past sin that has been dealt with.

Examine yourself. Do you hold a grudge against someone in your house? If you do, remember that Jesus already paid the penalty for whatever that person did wrong. Your inability to forgive belies your love. In fact, if a lack of forgiveness is characteristic of your life, you may not be a Christian.

Inevitably, those who have the greatest sense of forgiveness are quickest to forgive others. The people who know they've been forgiven much are able to forgive much. I hope that's true of you.

Ephesians 4:32 says, "Be kind to one another, tenderhearted, forgiving one another, even as God in Christ forgave you." God was kind and tenderhearted toward you, forgiving you even when you didn't deserve it. If you base your attitude toward people on what they deserve, you've missed the point. Don't yell at people, slander them, or get angry with them, even if they deserve it. Those who exemplify God's character are loving, kind, tender, and forgiving. That's the kind of attitude God expects from those who are His new creations in Christ.

PEACEFUL RELATIONSHIPS

Romans 12:18 urges, "Live peaceably with all men."

By definition, a peaceful relationship cannot be one-sided. You must do your part to make sure that your side of a relationship is right. Your inner desire, with God's help, should be to live in peace with everyone, even the most sinful, hard-to-get-along-with people.

Short of compromising the Word of God, you ought to extend yourself to great lengths to build peaceful bridges to those who persecute you and hate you. If you set aside any grudge or bitterness and from the heart completely forgive your enemies, you can honestly seek reconciliation with them.

LIVING THE MESSAGE

Paul stated clearly how we should live: "Whatever you do in word or deed, do all in the name of the Lord Jesus, giving thanks to God the Father through Him" (Colossians 3:17).

Unbelievers might pay more attention to our gospel message if we gave them something special to notice. We could start by not lying and always speaking the truth. What if we never became angry in a sinful way but always acted in love; never stole but always shared; and never spoke in a coarse manner but always spoke edifying words? Can you imagine how the lost might react if we never were bitter, wrathful, resentful, violent, or slanderous but were always characterized by kindness, tenderheartedness, and forgiveness?

Perhaps they would pay more attention then. Examine your own actions. Do you speak the truth? Do you have control over your anger so that it operates only in righteousness? Do you share your resources with others? Do you speak graciously? Are you kind, tenderhearted, and forgiving? If you are a new man or woman in Christ, you will live like that.

The greatest measuring rod of love in the life of a Christian may be forgiveness. That's because God showed His love to us in terms of forgiveness. The Bible could have taught us that God so loved the world that He made pretty flowers or trees or mountains. But it teaches that "God so loved the world that He gave His only begotten Son, that whoever believes in Him should not perish but have everlasting life" (John 3:16).

He gave His Son to forgive us. That certainly shows God's love more than flowers, trees, or mountains.

Measure your love. Ask yourself, *Do I love?* If you don't, you are not one of God's own because the children of God love others (1 John 4:7–8). How can you know whether you are characterized by love? Ask yourself, *Am I bitter toward someone because of something he did to me? Do I often get angry with people, either externally or internally? Do I speak maliciously behind people's backs?* Those are characteristics of your old lifestyle—characteristics you must get rid of in order to love and forgive *others*.

FOR THOSE HARD TO FORGIVE

Jesus is our example, and He "did not threaten" in the face of incredible suffering (1 Peter 2:23). He was spit on, His beard was pulled out, a crown of thorns was crushed onto His head, and nails were driven through His flesh to pin Him to a cross. In any other person, such unjust treatment would have caused feelings of retaliation to well up and burst out, but not Christ. He was the Son of God—creator and sustainer of the universe, holy and sinless—with the power to send His tormentors into eternal flames.

Yet Jesus never threatened His executioners with impending judgment; instead He forgave them. "Father, forgive them, for they do not know what they do" (Luke 23:34).

Christ died for sinners, including those who persecuted Him. He knew the glory of salvation could be reached only through the path of suffering, so He accepted His suffering without bitterness, anger, or a spirit of retaliation. May you respond as well to your suffering.

LET GOD HANDLE IT

The apostle Peter instructed Christians not to be "returning evil for evil or reviling for reviling, but on the contrary blessing" (1 Peter 3:9). That was Jesus' attitude. He was able to do that because He "committed Himself to Him who judges righteously" (2:23). The word translated as "committed" means "to hand over for someone to keep." In every instance of suffering, our Lord handed over the circumstance and Himself to God. That's because He was confident in the righteous judgment of God and the glory that would be His. That confidence allowed Him to accept tremendous suffering calmly.

That's the way you should respond when confronted with unjust persecution on the job or in your families or other relationships. When you retaliate, you forfeit the blessing and reward that suffering is meant to bring. Retaliation shows you lack the confidence you ought to have in God's ability to make things right in

His own time, which will include punishing the unjust and rewarding those who are faithful in suffering. So give it over to God and let Him handle it.

SUMMARY OF FORGIVENESS

No amount of tears can atone for sin. No number of good deeds can make amends for wrong we have done against God. No quantity of prayer or personal devotion can extenuate our guilt or cover it in any way. Even everlasting burning in hell will not purify the soul from sin. In the human realm there is nothing in time or eternity that can free us from the guilt of our sin. Those who seek a do-it-yourself solution to the problem of sin only shackle themselves all the more securely to their guilt.

Moreover, the smallest sin is so exceedingly vile that God—despite His infinite mercy, grace, and forgiveness—will not and cannot overlook even one sin without exacting its full penalty.

The only way to find real forgiveness and freedom from our sin is through humble, contrite repentance. We can't escape guilt by telling ourselves we are really not that bad. We must come face-to-face with the exceeding sinfulness of our sin.

The blood of Christ cries for forgiveness. Christ's atonement fully satisfied the demands of God's righteousness, so forgiveness and mercy are guaranteed to those who receive Christ in humble, repentant faith. We accept the responsibility for our sin, and also believe God that in the death of Christ sin is forgiven. We confess our sin so that the Lord can cleanse our conscience and give us joy (1 John 1:9).

NOTES

Chapter 1: We Need to Be Forgiven

1. "Compulsive Gambling May Be a Handicap, and a Shield from Firing," *Wall Street Journal* (June 21, 1988), 1.

2. Stanton Peele, *Diseasing of America* (Lexington, MA: Lexington Books, 1989), 2–4 (emphasis in original).

3. Bernie Zilbergeld, *The Shrinking of America* (Boston: Little, Brown, 1983), 89.

4. Ibid., 167.

5. Charles J. Sykes, *A Nation of Victims: The Decay of the American Character* (New York: St. Martin's, 1992), 13.

6. Wendy Kaminer, *I'm Dysfunctional, You're Dysfunctional* (Reading, MA: Addison-Wesley, 1992), 121.

7. Ibid., 124.

8. Ibid., 124–25.

9. Ibid., 20.

10. Ibid., 18.

11. Garth Wood, *The Myth of Neurosis* (New York: Harper & Row, 1986), 9.

Chapter 5: God Acts to Forgive

1. Kenneth E. Bailey, *Finding the Lost Cultural Keys to Luke 15* (St. Louis: Concordia, 1992), 110, 164.

ABOUT THE AUTHOR

Widely known for his thorough, candid approach to teaching God's Word, John MacArthur is a popular author and conference speaker and has served as pastor-teacher of Grace Community Church in Sun Valley, California, since 1969. John and his wife, Patricia, have four grown children and fifteen grandchildren.

John's pulpit ministry has been extended around the globe through his media ministry, Grace to You, and its satellite offices in seven countries. In addition to producing daily radio programs for nearly 2,000 English and Spanish radio outlets worldwide, Grace to You distributes books, software, audiotapes, and CDs by John MacArthur.

John is president of The Master's College and Seminary and has written hundreds of books and study guides, each one biblical and practical. Bestselling titles include *The Gospel According to Jesus*, *The Truth War*, *The Murder of Jesus*, *Twelve Ordinary Men*,

Twelve Extraordinary Women, and *The MacArthur Study Bible,* a 1998 ECPA Gold Medallion recipient.

For more details about John MacArthur and his Bible-teaching resources, contact Grace to You at 800-55-GRACE or www.gty.org.

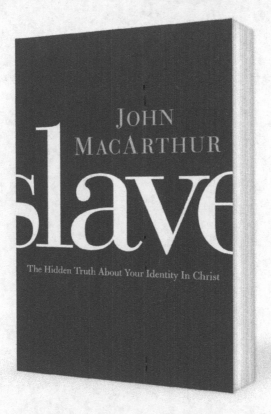

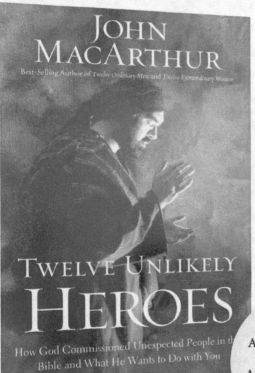

Printed in the USA
CPSIA information can be obtained
at www.ICGtesting.com
JSHW031628301223
54379JS00007B/36